"Joe Fisher is one of those rare souls ' n at
the same time, and occasionally he nι
grateful (mostly). Highly recommende. .

Jeff Lucas: author, speaker & broadcaster
www.jefflucas.org

"The wonderful thing about this lovely collection of poems is the way they
show so many sides of Joe. You probably know the Silly Jumper Joe. And
there is plenty of Silly Jumperness here. (Not least in the title!) But this book
also gives you the Reflective Joe, the Wondering, Pondering Joe, and the
Often Quite Moving Joe. It's a bargain, really. All the Joe's in one!"

Bob Hartman: storyteller, writer & entertainer

"A mighty collection of mini wonders. Joe will make you laugh and think and
ponder and love this creation we're in a bit more. Joe is a poet and I didn't
even know it; the Man on the Mic is also the Man with the Bic. (That's a pen.)
What a skill he has, helping see the world and its Creator through fresh eyes.
Uplifting and joyous, this is an excellent collection of inspirational poetry.
Highly recommended to everyone who knows words. Joe knows loads, and
he's gifted with them."

Paul Kerensa: scriptwriter, comedian & author
@paulkerensa

"Unsurprisingly, this book is much like Joe: funny, thoughtful, wise and witty. A
great creative resource but equally fantastic to read for pleasure. I'm sure this
book will bring joy to many people."

Cathy Madavan: writer, speaker, coach
and author of 'Digging for Diamonds'

Contents

This book is dedicated to my publisher,
Mark McKnight at McKnight & Bishop Ltd.

I wanted to dedicate it to my beautiful wife, Emma
and my two awesome offspring: Sam and Ellie.

But Mark threatened me, saying he would change it in the final edit
or at least redact my thoughts beyond all recognition.

I think this shows a staggering amount of ▌▌▌▌ ▌▌
and proves that Mark is nothing but a
▌▌▌▌▌▌▌▌▌▌▌▌▌▌▌▌▌▌▌▌▌▌▌▌

But whatever.

Here you go, Mark – finally you get a book dedicated to you.
I hope you're happy!

But seriously! The thankyous are endless and this couldn't be done
without the help and support of my friends and family, Emm and the kids,
my dad, Ted Fisher for his unending wisdom, support and encouragement.
Marc Kersalke who pushed me to start writing and Esther (the wonderful
Mother-in-law (I bet that isn't said often!!) who commissioned my
first piece for a carol service and set the ball rolling!
And all those over the years who have kept me going!
I'm still going!

Oh, and many blessings on you and yours! (see poem, Jargon-aught)

Preface

Joe Fisher is a performance poet and general speaker of the spoken word as opposed to any other kind of speaking. Known as The Man on the Mic, Joe works ~~tiresomely,~~ tirelessly around the UK, performing, speaking and speaking a little more, in events, theatres, sport and various other places where you can speak.

'The word POETRY can often conjure up many different feelings and attitudes. For many it's irrelevant and boring full of jargon and gobbledygook, a dead in the water art form that's dull and old fashioned and should be left in the past. Well not any more. Joe Fisher breathes modernity, humour, vulnerability and rhythm into his work. Much of his work is 'rap like'; maybe we should rephrase it 'rappetry'.

His subjects and ideas are on point and tug at the heart of life. His style his witty, biographical and often unpredictable with changes in pace and rhythm but always challenging and memorable. A diversity of subjects are covered from faith, equality, loss, fame, broken dreams, mental health, to the hatred of celery and the pain of being bald. This collection of spoken word poems are to be read aloud and performed. So go for it.

Or listen to joe performing some of them at You Tube/joetrypoetry

Even better why not book Joe to come and perform his poetry which can be created to suit your event in themes and style or a self contained poetry and comedy show!
See [f]acebook.com/joetrypoetry for more info

Faith, Hope & Nudity is his first printed work.
www.joefisher.net | @themanonthemic

When you put the word nudity into the title of a faith based book, you are asking for trouble. This was deliberate, a play off the phrase Faith, Hope and Unity!
The word nudity may conjure up all sorts of images and thoughts you may not want to be conjured up, or even considered but it's in nudity that new clothes can be given, in the vulnerability of life ,God comes. More of this later!!!

FAITH

Faith is one of those words that is used regularly within many contexts! For me, its about my walk with God, trusting despite proof and having a relationship with my creator! Many of these poems are prayers or psalms, but some are frank and honest about walking with God in life!

Faith, Hope & Nudity

Lord, restore my faith in only you.
Forgive the way I've trusted
In plans that never satisfy,
for things that die, I've lusted after,
giving everything I have
for that quick buzz,
that rush of blood,
that ego boost,
that sudden flood of pleasure.
Then I'm feeling good
but never lasts for long
and leaves a longing
stronger than before.
But you're the only hope I have.
Remove the things
that hold me back,
selfish desires
and schemes that lack
In substance and attack
the fundamental parts
of who I am.
Please bring abundance
of your grace
and show your mercy
for mistakes that rob me
of my place in all you have.
Then strip me of the rags
that cling, removing everything
that smells and dwells.
Then clean my skin
and all that grime
that's held within.
It will involve
some nakedness,

but that is what
you need to do.
Until you clothe me
with your love
and bring an outfit,
covering up my
pain and vulnerability.
You show your generosity
that cannot come
from anyone but you
So do this now.
I know I must allow
you all of me
so you can bring fluidity
that lives with faith
and lives with hope
and even sometimes nudity.

This is of course the title poem where I got the idea for the book.

I wanted to subvert this, as nudity is that place of letting yourself not matter (embarrassment, shame, vulnerability) in order to put someone else first (true love)

Nudity is a word that conjures up images that we'd often rather not approach but it evokes vulnerability and openness. the kind that we need if we are to be effective christians.

The famous phrase is Faith, Hope, and Unity (Love) the 3 theological virtues of Faith.

Faith Is A Doing Word

Faith is believing what you know you can't prove
but your faith can get flabby if you don't make it move.
It's one thing to know but another to do
and the thought without action is not good for you.

You see, faith needs an outlet like birds need the sky.
If you don't flap your wings, you're not gonna fly
and you're never getting fit if you just lie about
without moving your body and not getting out
of the norm or the humdrum you won't see an outcome
your limbs will go numb, if your sat on your........thumb.

Faith without works is like something that's died,
it won't grow or flourish if you keep it inside
and what is a groom if he loses his bride
and what is the sea if it loses its tide.
Faith without action's like a joint with no traction,
a head with no neck or a geek with no tech,
a window with no glass or solids without mass.
Like a star with no trek, or Ant without Dec.

Jesus calls us to do all the things that he did.
To heal, empower, to love and to give
everything that we have and not just a bit.
We can't have his light and keep it unlit
we can't have a signal and never transmit
we have to be real, we have to admit.
We can't say I do and then never commit.

Moving forward in faith will help us prevail,
if we fail to act, we then act to fail.
Faith mixed with works can help us to sail
through the storms and the waters
doing what Jesus taught us.
Being loyal supporters and changing our world.

This piece was written for a brief based on the 2017 Spring Harvest theme of 'Only The Brave'

I took the theme from James ,of 'faith without works' being dead and useless and I built upon that premise. I particularly like the pairs of things that correspond with faith and works.

I had to have Ant without Dec, (they're a presenting duo on TV, if you haven't heard of them). Then a few months later, Ant stopped working with Dec temporarily whilst on rehab! How spooky is that!!!

So we must practise what we preach
and live out what we teach.
Then faith comes alive
and empowers us to reach out
to those who are broken with horrors unspoken.
The angry, the hurting, the lost and the searching,
the lonely, the grieving, when life has no meaning.
The ones who are needing a new way to cope.
The ones who are sliding down a long and slippery slope.
The ones feeling helpless and need a new hope.

So we say it or we live it, these choices we choose.
We can take it or give it, just what can we lose?
Well, our faith if we don't use it will die out and fade,
so with God we are fearless.
We're only the brave.

The Two Me's

There are two me's you know,
two parts of the whole.
The me of the flesh
and the me of the soul.
There's the me who is broken,
and the me who is fixed.
The me who is focussed,
and the me who is mixed
up with worry amidst
the complete fear of life
eclipsed by anxiety,
sadness and strife.
There's the me who is bold,
and the me who has doubts.
The me who is peaceful,
and the one who just shouts
at the clouds and the darkness
and never quite knows
who the me really is
when insecurity shows.

It's up to myself now,
to choose who I'll be.
The me who is bound
or the me who is free.
The me who is blind,
 or the me who can see
way beyond all the nonsense
with true clarity.
The me who is prideful
and thinks he knows best.
The me who's a victim,
or the me who feels blessed.
The me who is guilty,
or the me with no shame

The me who's forgiven
and released from the blame

It's time to be me
who's no longer in chains,
to let go of me
that still wallows in pain
to find the true version,
that lives the good news.
In God I am certain,
that's the me that I choose.

Have you ever felt
torn in two? This is
especially true for
Christians. The Bible
talks about the flesh
life and the kingdom
life. I often feel this
pull between what I
naturally feel and
what I know I should
and could be.

Authentically Me

Unconditionally
recondition me.
Revive me
and transition me.
Take me from the mundane
into the extraordinary.
Make me the best
that I can be,
to flee from anonymity.
From doubt and insecurity
to know the truth,
to know I'm free.
To know my true identity.

Renew me
and
pursue me.
I no longer will conform
to uniformity
and norm.
But instead,
will be the true me,
removing all deformity.
I will outperform
upon a new platform,
of grace
and
true humility.

ke
ings
flow
oth in
ords and
life.This
ayer came out
a desire for
thenticity and
onesty. A need to
e real and genuine
a world that puts on
asks and expects to be
mething that we are
ot.

om a purely aesthetic
erspective, I wanted
at flowing sense that
mes from words with
soft sound that marry
th that flow of a life
th God.

I'm dissatisfied
not gratified,
without you
I'm against the tide.
I've tried, but on my own
I am nothing
but alone.
I want to hide, reside, abide, confide.
Be tied to you
and own the truth
that I am more
than meets the eye.
That I am yours,
that I can fly

Transform me
and inform me,
bring about a
perfect storm in me.

God the Boss

Imagine God as a surgeon.
He cuts and repairs.
Doing deep tissue healing,
and mending the tears.
His word cutting deep,
his truth like a knife,
that takes out the tumours
and fixes my life.
Yet we question the treatment
and can't take the strain.
We don't have the patience,
and don't want the pain
that's required for the healing,
it's just not appealing,
and causes ill feeling,
which hinders the gain.

Imagine God as bus driver.
He drives me around,
knowing all the best
detours, whilst heading
homebound.
Yet we don't trust his driving
and beg to get off
halfway through the excursion,
even though there's more stops.
We don't trust his leading
and think we know best,
we grab hold of the wheel
as we think hat he's messed up
the right navigation,
or missed the last station,
we show aggravation,
we're so not impressed!

We constantly accept peoples roles in life and trust them to do their jobs but seem to find it really hard to accept God's role as boss and chief!

Imagine God as head teacher.
The boss of the school.
The one that we follow,
the one with the rules.
Yet we question his actions
and walk out of class,
we think we know better
and don't want to ask,
for his knowledge and
teaching,
we don't like the preaching
but we'll never be reaching
those goals, we won't pass!

You would never walk out
whilst you're having an op.
You would not leave the bus,
before it could stop.
You'd not tell the head
teacher he's no longer the boss.
Yet we do it so often,
with the one we call God.

It's time to believe that God
won't leave us scarred.
That his surgery's worth it
and our hearts he will guard.
We must trust that he knows us,
and knows where to go.
That he won't leave us stranded
or leave us alone.
We must let him be head
over all that we are.
He'll give us the answers,
its better by far,
to just let him be sovereign
and let him be king.
Over life, over all,
over everything!

You are I am

Have you ever felt meaningless, useless, unwise and weak? I know have.

This poem was written in that place of being close to self pity.

Close to feeling like I wasn't
able to be anything better or do anything better. It's often a good place to be as God can move in and be the I AM

I'm not wise.
I'm not focused.
I'm not steady.
I'm not clear.
I'm not righteous.
I'm not perfect.
I'm not present.
I'm not here.
I'm not generous.
I'm not giving.
I'm not loving.
I'm not fair.
I'm not knowing it.
I'm not getting it.
I'm not full of it.
I'm not there.
I'm not graceful.
I'm not peaceful.
I'm not gentle.
I'm not pure.
I'm not truthful.
I'm not thoughtful.
I'm not confident.
I'm not sure.
I'm not beautiful..
I'm not stunning
I'm not epic.
I'm not glam.
I'm not joyful.
I'm not awesome.

But You are
So I am!

As a Christian, I can be confident that whatever I am not

God is!

His 'I am'
out does
my nots
or Knots!

15

Holy Joe

They call me Holy Joe,
but I wholly wonder why?
As I'm wholly imperfect
and wholly I'm quite sly.
I'm totally unholy,
and sometimes I'm not fair.
But slowly,
I'm wholly, becoming aware,
that I could
become holy,
but not if I try.
It cannot be earned
and I certainly can't buy It,
or get it myself
as It's given quite freely,
there's no need for wealth,
I just need to be needy.
To wholly give in,
to the saviour
who sees me
as holy, because,
on the cross,
he has freed me.
So wholly right now,
I'm implored to be holy,
by grace and forgiveness
and mercy that shows me,
that life can be different.
I don't need to be lonely
I'm free to now enter
the Holy of Holies!

Holiness is a strange word so I decided to pursue the words Holy and Wholly.

I do get called Holy Joe by those friends of mine who are not religious.

This is a nice play on words with wholly and holy!

D Minus

Deceived
and distracted.
Diverted,
deployed.
Damaged,
detracted.
Deterred and
destroyed.

Demoted,
dejected.
Defamed
and denied.
Degraded,
deflected,
deluded,
deprived.

Dreadfully depressed.
Despairingly desolate.
Deliriously dense.
Dutifully desperate.

Drastically dangero'us.
Dauntingly dumb.
Directly deluded.
Deceptively done.

Downhearted,
disgruntled.
Dissed and
displaced.
Discarded,
deluded,
declined and
disgraced.

Disobedient,
depressive.
Disloyal
and dazed.
Diminished,
detested
demeaned
and delayed.
I'm defiantly definite,
that darkness and dread,
will dine here no longer,
divine defeats death.

Distinguished,
discerning,
dependant
devout.
Decisive,
devoted,.
Death beaten,
no doubt.

The dross and the damage
can do one and die
defeated the darkness, delivered am I.

I've had a few D Minus
marks in my time. The idea here
was to take all the negative
words beginning with D that I
could think of, then minus them
from the picture and juxtapose
them with the positive ones.

I love 'Death beaten, no doubt'

Proud of that line!

17

No Chance

When,
you've been treated bad
or are wrongly dismissed.
When the punch of betrayal
hits you like a fist.
Whilst revenge tends to court you,
with lips that are kissed.
Then forgiveness won't be,
at the top of your list

For it's our nature to say
'I can never forgive'
'I was wronged and mistreated
and I'm ready to live,
with the actions of hatred,
it is what it is'
But where will it leave you?
Alone and amiss?

'Got to get myself even,
to settle the score'
No thought of repentance.
'Please God will you pour
out your vengeance on them.

They totally deserve it,
they hurt me and bruised me,
you know, you observed it.

The truth is however,
we must try to let go
of all of that pain
it might kill us you know,
or make us feel bitter,
so that we never grow,
into all that is promised,
the peace and the flow of
a true love thats offered
from one that does know
the true cost of forgiveness,
he did it just so.

Jesus gave up his life,
and forgave those that killed him.
He also did this, so we are forgiven.
His strength will enable us.
If we allow,
he'll help us to forgive
and he will show us how.

One of the main themes of the Christian faith is Forgiveness and it's one of the toughest concepts to get our heads around. I still struggle with it as it goes against all our natural impulses to get even. As a Christian though I know I must do as Jesus did, forgive, forgive, forgive!

I Need a P Please God

I need a P please God?
But the P that I mean,
is not what you think.
As the P that I dream of
puts me on the brink of a
POWERFUL gift bringing
full kitchen sink,
and not just a phase
or a nod and a wink,
but a full flowing fountain
from which you can drink.
A life that is brimming,
a bright light not dimming,
no surface I'm skimming
no reason to shrink.

I long for the PRESENCE
of He who creates.
Who makes something,
from nothing,
who loves, never hates.
Brings true life,
love and blessings,
who stands at the gates of
a joy never ending,
of true love that waits.

I dream of the PASSION,
that leads me to live,
a life full of giving,
compels me to give,
give away all my fears,
and then calls me to
sieve out the dross
and the nonsense

adhere to the
conscience,
to know what
I've known
since this love narrative
was narrated by
Jesus
who helps me forgive.

I dream of the PEACE
that is clearly
bestowed.
From a God
that gives freely,
no toll on this road.
Where the calm,
defies logic
and shalom is
then sewed into
the heart of
my being
and nothing
is owed.

I hold to the PROMISE,
that never shall die.
That I'm loved,
by a lover,
who helps me to fly.
Fly away from
all darkness
and into the light
of a wonderful saviour
who helps me do right.

I dream of a PURPOSE,
a meaning of life.
A true and real calling,
that cuts like a knife.
A need to be needed,
a seed to be seeded,
a life not impeded by
trouble and strife
I long for a challenge,
that's made causable,
by a God of the epic
and implausible.
Who gives us a reason
and now calls us all,
to live undefeated,
mistakes not repeated,
the climb is completed,
and never shall fall.

The Powerful Presence,
the Passion, the Peace
Are the P's that
I need from
a God who releases
his Promise and
Purpose,
his love will increase,
giving hope
everlasting
and love that
won't
cease. Remember,
Blockbusters on
TV in the 1980's?
'Can I have a P please
Bob?' My take on that
phrase using as many P
words as I can think of!

Me, Myself and Thy

I stand in front of the mirror,
and I consider the face looking
back at me.
Who am I?
What makes me tick?
What do I see?
The true reflection or a distorted
version based on my experiences
and my identity?

My brain forms a picture of what
Is in front of my eyes.
It might as well be a fun fair mirror
looking back at me.
The twisted images of ugliness and
disfigurement are believed to be
reality.
Yet deception has won the battle
over the facts.
The truth is hidden by the glass.

'You knit me together
in my mother's womb.
I am fearfully and wonderfully made'
But something must have gone wrong,
as I'm fearful,
and don't feel particularly wonderful.
I'm not even sure sometimes,
If I was created or just a happy
accident.

Life and loss has misted up
the true image,
blocked the light coming through.
Lies have created

a different picture,
falsehood and fakery
have taken centre stage.
The world has offered me
a benchmark by which
I Judge myself by.
And judge myself, I do.

'You created my inmost being'
Yet my being is deceived.
I don't often see what you see.
I can't feel what you need me to
feel.
I',m sad, lost and abandoned,
afraid to truly open my eyes
and look within to see the true me.

'Your eyes saw my unformed body;
all the days ordained for me
were written in your book'
Yet what I see a deformed body and
an uninformed mind.
Most days, I don't even want to
look,
let alone know that I am loved,
redeemed,
planned for and valued.
Most days, its me, myself and I,
please let it be, me myself and Thy!

A rare non rhyming poem for me.
This is based on the Psalm 139!
'You created my inmost being'
and focuses on identity.

Sway

My mother used to rock me to sleep,
back and forth.
A simple and gentle movement.
A comforting movement.
Never vigorous,
or aggressive.
Never forceful,
or excessive.
Just gentle,
always gentle.
I never had to do anything,
but lie there and feel the sway.

I guess i need to remember
that I live in the arms,
of a true mother and father.
A Heavenly Father.
I feel his sway,
the mesmeric, hypnotic, relaxing sway.
The sway that says peace.
The sway that says all is well.
The sway that says let go,
there is nothing you can do.
You don't even need to move.
Just stay still and let him sway.
Yes let him sway
Yes, Let him have his way.

Inspired by a lullaby! Lets sway! Let him have his way!

Mindfulness

I don't mind,
If you
remind me
that my mind you must
renew.
As my mind it tends to wander,
a lost mind will just not do.
So I'll mind the gap,
reminded that,
you mind if I'm not mindful

and
my mind is blinded
by the world,
and tied to tongue.
So please unfurl,
those narrow minded
attitudes,
and unintended platitudes.
A cleaned up mind
I plan to choose.
Which helps me mind
my Ps and Qs

inspired by 'Mind the gap' on a London Tube!

Ever felt like you're not sure
where you are, 'Between a rock
and a hard place' is one phrase.
'No mans land' is another.

No Man's Land

I feel like I'm in no man's land,
with nowhere left to stand, without
the chance of losing limbs by moving,
choosing wrongly gets you hurt.
This scorched dark turf,
this damaged earth, has left its marks.
The enemy just marches through,
yet friendly fire has hurt me too and made
me doubt which side to choose.
The stray incendiaries lie in wait.
The scars of war, inflated by the pain of
life. It's lonely here and frightening.
As bullets fly and bombs ignite,
enlightening the darkened sky.
Nowhere to turn, it seems, as burning
promises and dreams, lie broken.
Man made schemes and hurts unspoken.
Yet, no mans land is as it says
and maybe that's the clue?
It's not man's land, but God's.
He made this world and knows
the pitfalls and the mines.
The darkest times, the barbed wire
pained him too.
And yet, he broke on through that barrier,
this warrior of heaven dwells here,
knowing where to tread.
He quells fear, carrying that dread for me.
Instead of leaving me for dead.
So no mans land may yet be where
I need to be right now,

allowing God to shelter me
and trusting, that he'll help me,
when it's needed,
not just when I feel it.
This war has made me rue the day,
but I can yet again let go,
and know he'll navigate the way.
A victory, he will instigate
as long as I'm prepared to wait
and trust he knows the plan.
So here in God's land,
I will stand
and put my life into his hands.

That's what inspired this piece
and considering the fact, that
if it's not man's place then
maybe that in-between is
where God dwells. The space
between, the barren land,
God is still there!

RE-

Repurpose,
resharpen,
refresh and renew.
Regarding my life,
please reshape and
resume.
Re-find me, rewind me
remind me of you.
I'll retry, re-apply,
I'll rely on the truth.
Revive, reawaken,
reboot and review,
who I am, where I am,
then remake and redo

Realign, redesign,
re-assign and remove, all the darkness,
the hardness, the stark residue.
Repossess, readdress,
re-access where I've been.
Re-equip and resource,
then reverse what I've seen.
Remove the rebuking,
regret and remorse.
Reduce all the worry,
release and resource me,
when reeling from heartache.
Reform and then remake.
Rework all the workings,
reward and then retake
my life, from the rubble.
Rebuild, burst the bubble.
Release me from trouble and all of the pain.
Reset and reseal, react and reveal,
all the things that are broken,
reform and re-heal.

Increase the reflection, reduce the rejection,
bring true resurrection from all that was dead.
Re-alight, reignite, reunite and re-write,
and make sure I recite
all the things that bring light.
You've removed all the shame,
so reclaim and rename
all the things left unspoken.
Rekindle the flame.
You're the reason I live,
so give life once again
and my all I will give,
cause in you I remain.

How many words that start with the prefix or the letters RE can I fit into a poem?

I have no idea as I've not counted, but there are lots and its a prayer for renewal and many more things beginning with RE words!

23

This My Prayer

At the start of this new day,
dear Lord I ask and pray,
that you will hold me fast
and stay
beside me,
and your hand will hold
and guide me,
through the troubles
and the times,
where worries
still divide my mind.
Give me your whisper of delight,
and those warm arms
that hold me tight,
and don't let go,
throughout the night,
when darkness
tries to hide my light.
I'll trust in you and
trust that you will bring me through
the pain
and all confusion,
Into all that you
have promised.

Make me truthful,
make me honest.
Make me humble,
keep me on this
narrow road.
Never forgetting,
what is owed by
all the love
that you've bestowed
on me, despite my sin
and forgery,
you've loved me and
forgiven me.
So now I see humility,
and hold on to
you, day by day,
relying on stability
that only comes from you.
And here will stay
within your arms and
never stray or be alarmed.
Cause you are mine and I am yours,
for now Lord and for evermore
Amen.

•

I wanted to write something that was simply a prayer,
to start each day. I hope that's what I achieved

Continuing the easter theme. my aim here was to see resurrection as the next part of the story and how we as Christians, get caught up in guilt and shame and forget that God can beat death and sin and bring resurection.

Stuck at the Cross

What does God have to do
to get me to see,
that I'm already saved,
that I'm already free.
Yet I live life defeated,
ashamed and alone,
so scared of my shadow,
undone and unknown.
Unsure and uncertain,
unable to show any backbone
or courage
or anything close.
Unnervingly,
under a cloud
that has thrown
underwhelming
amounts of unbearable rain.
Being blown,
from one place to another,
I'm prone,
to again give up trying
and live with the pain,
even though

we've been mended,
sin taken away,
freedom's intended,
this is a new day.
God's mercies are free,
but we're riddled with shame.
We've got a new hope,
but we live with the same
old thoughts and obsessions,
repeating transgressions,
recalling confessions,
requesting possessions,
repressing expressions,
rehearsing impressions,
repelling concessions,
receiving oppressions,
reliving depressions,
reversing progressions,
relenting discretion's,
revealing repressions.
We're stuck at the cross,
in the mess, blood and gore,
but must get past the grief,
we forget what its for.
We ignore resurrection
and stay on the floor,
instead of imploring
our hearts to restore,
the love that we had
and knowing there's more.
Death beaten, sin broken,
God has settled the score.
He's given new life
by sending his Son.
So lets live in the victory
The battle is won!

The Jargon-aught

Watch out cause the
Jargon-aught's coming.
Created to keep you in tow.
A head on collision,
with words that are weird,
you'll be flat,
if you're not in the know.
The jargon is there,
as a way to belong.
You feel very special,
when you have your own song.
But no one can sing it,
they can't play along.
They don't know,
the words and
the tune sounds all wrong.
'Sanctification'
'sin' and 'damnation'
'redeemed', 'justified'
'our hope of salvation'
'The spirit is moving'
'I'll give Him my heart'
'unburden your burdens'
'we are set apart.'
These are fabulous phrases
and wonderful words,
to those who have learnt them,
but to others absurd!
'Washed in the blood' sounds
quite gory and dumb.
To be 'born again'
would be bad for your mum.
'My heart is ablaze'
wow that really must hurt,
the fire brigade,
I will call and alert.
'Its time now to share'.
What are we sharing? With who?
'A hedge of protection'
A tree won't save you.
'I am feeling led'
that's a strange thing to do.
I'm walking with God,
ooh, can I please come too?
It's exclusive, reclusive,
not very inclusive,
or even conducive to true openness.
It can be so obtrusive,
elusive, abusive,
not useful to those
who just want to progress.
So lets think about,
all of the things that we say.
Our words are important,
they can show folks the way.
Or they can be a blockage
to what God can do,
so beware of the Jargon-aught
it might just get you.

One of my greatest bug bears with Church culture is jargon! It can be so off putting to people exploring faith when they feel excluded, and jargon does that. I like the concept of this massive truck that has no sensitivity and is only for those that are 'in the know.' I call it the Jargon-Naught!

26

Time To Talk

I gave my wife a list today.
Just some suggestions fairly plain.
I think you'll get the gist,
of what i mean when
I explain, that
it was full of ways
that she could show me

just how much she's loves and knows me.
Going and bestowing on me,
gifts of generosity,
with openness and honesty,
with passion and velocity.
Giving ME just what i need,

but honestly,
that's not what
I received.
Just total animosity!

It doesn't take a genius,
to work out what came next.
She was perplexed and vexed,
my selfishness and needs,
are met without the keenness,
to then invest in her,
it's stressful.
Yes.

I guess it's cause I offered nothing
in return for my demands,
of dreams and plans that might occur.
To that she did infer.
'A one way road does not allow a two way
thing when ones way's closed.
A duo cannot sing alone
there's no way this is happening'.

For some,
this might be how we pray.
A wish list, you could say,
that's left at heavens door
without a thought of what
we offer in return and yet
God yearns to give us good things,

when we open up our,
hearts and minds.
A true relationship
combines the
talking and the listening,
not just producing lists

and then expecting gifts.
Or glistening the juicy bits,
but not the graft,
It's daft,
to not give back
as after all we're his.

This love is not a tit for tat thing,
but a true love at
all costs thing.
Saved from loss,
Jesus, his cross has offered,
intimacy.

Talk to God he's listening
but listen back,
and see that he has so much
that he wants to say.
This prayer can be unlimited,
no barriers, no walls today
His grace allows us access
to a God that has it all.

And says come close and be my friend.
Let's chat!
There is no end to that,
no rubbish signals
never sending,
nuisance calls,
or now unfriending.

True connection is here.
He's near.
No pending slips,
are necessary,
he waits to answer.
Let's be ready

Open up your mouth,
and speak,
whilst seeking God, and what he'll say.
And into heaven we will peek,
It's time to talk,
right now!

Let's pray.

Written specifica
for Spring Harvest 20
on the theme of Pra
being Unlimi

HOPE

What we do think of when we think of hope?
We think, of a new day, new start, new life!
Laughter gives hope, so some of these poems
are fun, silly and comedic and others just give
us a sense of hope, I HOPE you like them!

Every Little Helps

Every little helps,
but when clearing the shelves,
It's now self service!
So they're helping themselves.

BOGOF

She leaves me the list
then the rest I must fess,
Is all up to guesswork
at best Its a test, that I've listened,
Invested and glistened the info.
So I'm grabbing my hessian.
I'm certainly no hero.
But the question is whether
I'll cause a transgression
or mess up this session
of shopping,
investing in hopping through aisles.
Oh yes its depressing!
I'll always keep stressing,
this job is my Everest.
I'm just not the best at this,
too blokey you know
and forgetting one thing
will leave me alone
with my ego suspended from string,
high or low.
So I had better be right,
or I'm not coming home.

Shopping!
AGGHHH!

Maybe it's a
bloke thing,
but nothing
makes me
more stressful
than a busy
supermarket!

So on with the job
all armed and prepared.
My dignity spared with
arms full of bags.
'These ones are for life',
my conscience then brags.
'Don't buy anymore',
it also then nags.
Then into the brink,
with the throngs and the crowds,
It's time to switch on and
start spending the pounds,
whilst looking for bogofs
and plenty of rounds,
of bananas,
but loose,
or in packets I think,
yellow or green,
or ones in the shrink
wrap, thats plastic,
forget it!
I'm not going there.
Just place in the basket
and prove that you care.
This is just the beginning,
I've selected one thing,
and still need a trillion,
all on a shoestring.
Then I'll go with my instinct,
buy sweet tooth delights,
I'm glad that this market
is open all night,

but it doesn't feel Super,
as I'm lost in a queue
to grab
all that is needed,
then off to the loo.
Then the cafe
the phone shop,
the late pharmacy,
the tailors, the kiosk
the fresh bakery.
I'm going quite crazy
and possibly
mad.
The truth is upon me,
I shop like my dad!
No care for what's written,
just swooned by a sale
even if i don't need them
I love a cheap rail.
With bargains galore
and plenty of stuff,
more than one trolley
is never enough.
I'm going stir crazy,
can't keep up with this,
there's too many choices,
especially the crisps!
So now to go home,
and get back the time.
I may just give in
and
do it online.

7 Seconds

7 seconds, they say
is all that you need,
to decide what you think
you are thinking of me.
It's subconscious,
at best,
I must stress and impress,
first impressions are
vested, expressed
and ingested,
addressed and digested
redressed
and contested.
In no time at all,
I've been judged
and then tested
no room for inquest,
if I've messed
up my chance,
that impression
is there from
that very first glance.
No rehearsal, reversal
or any advance.
I must live with the image,
assumption and stance,
that I left there
unrivalled,
unable to change,
what you think I am like,
I just can't rearrange.
So whatever the setting,
whatever the place.
I must do my best
be amazing,
with grace,

be engaging,
breath taking,
be funny,
be fair.
Be active,
attractive,
proactive,
with flair.
Be charming,
a darling,
disarming,
aware,
that whoever
I'm meeting,
no seconds to spare.
So I will do my all,
to be cool from the start.
In the first seven seconds
I'll be sure I don't fart!

The prem
for this was h
quick we can ma
an impression on peop
the argument is that i
between 4 & 7 secor
First impressions cou

Cliche Away

When push comes to shove,
at the end of the day.
You're never too far,
from a phrase or cliché.
They might make you cringe,
and needless to say.
I'll never avoid
this lazy word play.
I'll work like a dog
but It's not what you think,
I'm throwing in everything,
but the kitchen sink!
So live and let live,
in the blink of an eye.
Let's cut to the quick,
with a word to the wise.
These cliches are starting
to skate on thin ice!
The undeniable truth,
words are naughty but nice.
Forgive and forget
and play your cards right!
Cause maybe my bark
is worse than my bite.
I'm now flying solo,
right into the night,
but with blue sky thinking,
I'm as high as a kite.
You assume that these phrases
will clear the whole room,
but assume makes an ass
out of you,
and of me.
I've thousands of these.
I'm armed to the teeth

I went to a poetry workshop when I first started writing, and was told to avoid cliches!

So I decided to face the issue head on and write a poem that was chock full of them!

I believe that there are 54 well known cliches!

Count them!

There may be more!

33

whatever you say,
I've an ace up my sleeve.
I'll land on my feet.
Get these lines off my chest.
Even if I'm mutton that's,
dressed
as a lamb.
But there's no I in team.
We are family.
I hope I'm not barking,
up the wrong tree.
When all's said and done,
I need your attention.
Necessity is the mother,
of all invention.
It's clear as a bell,
that I've no hope in hell,
even when wishing,
all's well that ends well.
I'm older than my years,
so blood sweat and tears,
won't help as I'm
wet behind these ears.
So time to quit rhyming,
step outside the box,
or blow off some steam
and go the whole hog.
In a mad twist of fate,
I've got a clean slate

but remember good things
come to those who do wait.
As a matter of fact,
its too good to be true.
I've just bitten off
more than I can chew.
So it's time to take stock.
Whatever life brings.
These words are a few
of my favourite things.
So day in and day out,
I'll take it on the chin.
But it ain't really over
till the fat lady sings.
I'll cut to the chase
and say holy cow.
They think it's all over,
Guess what?

It is now.

Celery is Hellery!

Please,
don't start telling me
that celery is anything
but veggie hell
you see,
I've just never understood,
why you would think that it was
good.
It tastes of totally nothing,
Its a stick not made of wood!
'But its nice with
salad dressing
or with hummus'
But I'm guessing
that your stomachs
aren't that pleased.
As it certainly won't ease,
those current hunger pains or needs.
You see you might as well eat trees,
or something similar like leaves.
Even common garden peas

at least,
have something of a taste.
So please just bin it, do not waste
another minute
on this miniature green twig.
As its just made up of thin air
cause theres actually
nothing in it,
to acknowledge
or to solicit
any eating.
Just admit it.
You're not cheating anybody,
but your taste buds,
to pretend that it would taste good.
So I beg you,
to find something
that might humour us and bless us .
Yes I'm gonna ditch
This nonsense
And return to eating lettuce.

Sorry people, I have to honest! I cant bear celery!
The look, the taste, the point of it!
Here's a comedy poem based on the hatred of celery.
Just my opinion, but its comedy! Honest..

Mid life Chrysalis

Life starts at 40,
or 50 they say.
So that means,
that I've started,
but I'm not sure that they,
who delivered that line
knew quite what they meant.
As I don't feel their fervour,
or get their intent.
I'm hitting late 40's,
and Im feeling quite old.
But I'm just in the middle
or so I am told.
There's much more to come,
that's the story I'm sold,
but the stomach is spreading
and I'm already bald.
I now have to lift up my
glasses to see.
I moan, when I'm standing,
I'm tired by 3!
I even like smelling the Pot Pourri!
Will someone explain
what is happening to me?
I'm questioning life
and all that I've done,
I now take 6 tablets
where I used to take one.
I'm no longer wanting to
have as much fun!
Cause it's all too much hassle,
I may just unravel,
I'm stuck In my battle
and I don't think I've won.
I'm tired and jaded
Not knowing if, all this

Is making me bigger,
or bringing a smallness,
or pulling me under
and leaving a dullness.
I'm losing the wonder
of life in its fullness!
My get up and go,
just got up and went.
I want to invest but I'm empty
and spent.
I want to climb up,
but I'm on a descent.
I need a release,
but I've shut off the vent.
A mid life crisis!!!
I guess you might think?
I'm not playing the field,
or turning to drink.
Not buying a race car,
or sat on the brink
of a terrible breakdown.
Oh no I won't sink,
In that sea of depression,
or anything close.
It might be, they're right
I just need to see,
those,
new flowers that bloom.
A new start,
be reborn,
come out of the womb
and see a new dawn.
So it's time to break out
of the cocoon so tight,
and see the horizon
new eras,

new flight.
I'm going to embrace
the start of new things.
It's my mid life chrysalis.
I'm getting new wings!

I'm in my late 40s!
This, I guess leans towards a
mid life crisis!
I love the play on words!
New start, no crisis here;
just a chrysalis.

New life, new start, new wings!

Easter Haiku's

It took just three days
to go from darkness to light
forever I'm changed

On friday we mourn
whilst on Saturday we wait
Sunday he's alive

A Haiku is a
Japanese poem
with particular
style and
structure. These
two haiku's are
written for Easter!

The Beast from the East

This poem was
written in the midst
of the storms
battering Britain. I
wanted to relate
these to sin and the
Easter story,
beating sin through
the cross.

The beast from the east
will not feast here at Easter.
Defeated by Jesus,
deaths bleakness is beaten.
The cross will reprieve,
while deceit then decreases,
deletes the deceased
as the risen, released us.
Forgiveness unleashed
as the freedom increases,
his peace is revealed
bringing life in it's sweetness

Joyeux Noel

Zelig kerstfeest, Joyeux noel,
Felis natal, let all be well.
In any tongue,
It's Christmas time.
The seasons here,
the bells will chime.
The lights, the snow
the fun, the din.
Merry Christmas,
Let the joy the begin.

The winter sun that
shines so bright.
The squeals of joy,
the pure delight
The presents opened
 in the light.
The Christmas noise,
the silent night.
The joy of the nativity,
the dressing up,
the liberty,
of donkeys, kings and
all those things
that never were
but now will be
forever in festivity.

As Santa visits on his sleigh,
and ho, ho, ho!
He tends to say,
the fat man in a bright red hood
will give you toys if you are good.
But is this what we want to see,
a bribe to be a better me.

We pile the presents, and we breed,
the gluttony, whilst many bleed
In poverty and endless need.
But still we fail to hear and heed
the warning of a life of a greed.

For some, the season's full of pain.
The hurt and sadness still remain.
The darkness and the night sustain.
The awful memories rise again,
of empty lives
of love ones lost
the endless ache,
the counting cost,
of frozen hearts that don't defrost,
of fragile people simply tossed, away
and left to hope that just one day,
they might be alright
they might be ok.

Whilst in the manger,
full of hay, the little baby,
there does lay.
A sign for all humanity,
while most will hear, yet few will see.
That Jesus might just be the key,
to one day being found and free

And then that revolutionary,
did something,

that we must believe.
He broke the hold of sin and death
And then breathed a brand new breath.
of life,
that means that we are left,
to live again and there remain.
So whilst we sing and dec the halls,
receive the gift that's best of all
The gift of life, of love, of joy,
brought by that little baby boy.

This was the first poem that I wrote. Christmas 2017, as a request for a Christmas carol service.
A mix of the fun and frivolity of Christmas with the message of the true meaning of the festive season.

Hope Deferred

Hope deferred makes the heart sick.
Beating you up with a big stick.
Draining your soul and creating a hole,
which leaves you all cold and anaemic.

A love that is lost
leaves an oil slick that costs,
all you have to remove,
or it drops you in goo,
that you just can't undo,
like an illness, a flu
which leaves you, without
a desire or a clue,
that remains in your being
and then causes you,
to feel hurt and abandoned,
the sinking of sand
and the swell of a gland
that will grow and demand
all the strength of your heart,
all the works of your hand.

Dreams unfulfilled,
try to unstick your plans.
Throws a huge brick
that lands, at your heart,
then expands,
leaving damage,
that scans across time
and untangles your life,
leaving debris, and grime,
and a lie telling you,
that you're nothing, your none,
that there's nowhere to run,
that the light has now faded.

The darkness has won!

Yet a seed in some dung,
is a garden to some.
And a small glimpse of light
from someone who knows right,
might be all that you need
to insight
not impede
that release of a freedom,
that frees you to lead on
and lift up your head.
That implores you to spread
out your wings
and not focus on things
that will leave you in dread.
But instead,
will allow to tread
through the treacle,
to move to a sequel.
This might be a new chance,
you might leap, you might dance,

A new frame,
a new stance,
a new you that is equal
to all that you face.
That will free you to trace
out a new path,
a new dawn,
a new hope,
a new way,
a new life,
a new start,
a new love,
a new day.

Ever lost hop
ever felt like
all over? Yep, me t
The verse in Proverbs 13
Says, "Hope deferred mak
the heart sick but a longing fulfill
is a tree of l
This was written with new year in sig

Sugar!

I lost 0.2, just by having a poo.
If I think this one through
what more could I do.
I could weigh in the nude,
or wear some thin pants,
or change all the numbers
by changing my stance.

Yes, it's time to lose weight
and get rid of the fat,
but the truth is,
I'm lazy and terribly bad
at all of the fitness
the diets and that.
I'd rather sit still and
just cuddle the cat.
The fact I don't have one
just figures and shows
what lengths I will take
to put off what I know.

My circumference increases,
the belly, it grows,
I can't see my knees
and I can't see my toes.
It's true,
I'm obsessed,
with sugar and sweets.
I can't go a day,
without having a treat.
Be it chocolate,
or ice cream
or maybe a slice
or seven of cake,
that'll do me just right.

I should
probably
apologise for
my first line.
But I won't.
It's crass and
slightly
naughty but
stems from
chats with
dieters and
personal
experiences
of regularly
weighing
ourselves.

The first line
was heard by
a friend of
mine at a
slimming
club and
inspired the
poem!

You see my bloodstream
is buzzing,
with nothing but sugar,
its making me fuller,
and humming with vigour.
The trigger
is always the sweet,
not the salty?
maybe its true,
that my taste buds are
faulty.

I need to take action
and get right off my bum.
If I'm longing for sugar,
I' ll just take a run,
drink water more often,
less sweetness more veg.
A small piece of cake
instead of a wedge.
As long as I'm heathy
as long as I'm fit
I might have to accept
that it sticks out a bit.

So do I need to change,
or can I just find
a new sugar that's
healthy,
one that's refined,
or a new way of
weighing,
that might have to say,
as long as I'm healthy
I'm ok this way.

The next time I go,
to the world of the slim,
or the watchers of weight,
that will try make me thin.
I'm going to remember,
that if I'm ok within,
I might just get by
with the odd little syn!

You're an Oxy, I'm a Moron

You're beautifully brutal.
You're sharpishly blunt.
You're lovingly hateful.
You're quietly upfront.

I'm stupidly clever.
I'm awfully nice.
I'm anxiously calm,
I'm loosely precise.

You're deliberately random.
Courageously brittle.
Completely unfinished.
Massively little.,

I'm Intensely disinterested.
Totally not there.
Modestly arrogant.
I'm justly unfair.

We're slightly considerable.
We're unnervingly scared.
We're positively negative.
We're Individually paired.

A play on
the theme
of
Oxymorons!

An
Oxymoron is
a contra-
dictory
figure of
speech
which I've
put into the
context of a
relationship.
Each line is
an
Oxymoron!

Opposites
attract.

This is the
Extreme of
that.

Why?

Can you please explain why,
I've got nothing on top,
when the hairs from my nose
seem never to stop.
I've got nothing to show
and nothing will grow.
Where I'd love a long main,
no sign of a mop!
No hope of,
a dreadlock,
a mullet or bun.
There's no number 3 cut,
not even a 1.
No hope of a pony
or any such tail.
No hope of extensions,
they just won't prevail.
My side parting left all,
on the side and departed.
No effort at all, on the head
so half hearted,
no hair in my eyes
as the hair hasn't started.
I can't make it grow
cause the landscapes uncharted.
Yet the hair grows elsewhere
like tomorrow won't come.
They've a life of their own!
I won't mention the bum.
You see hairs seem to prosper
on all but my head,
they are living all over
but on top they're quite dead.
I'd love them right there,
but I'm stuck here instead,
With a face full of beard,

which is happy to spread,
but it's not where I want it.
No wash, just a go,
no conditioner needed,
no locks that will flow.
The hairdresser addressed,
the whole truth
and then stressed
that she'd have to impress
that I'm no longer blessed,
with the hairs on my head
that I'm naked, not dressed,
in an examination
I'd not pass the test.
She said it was hopeless
there's nothing to choose.
Not even a crew cut
there's no hair to do.
I could get a shine,
or a polish and buff.
I could wear a wig,
and go on with the bluff.
I could get a weave,
but there isn't enough
to tie onto or anchor,
the truth is its tough.
I'm a slap-head, a baldy,
I've nothing up there,
I' m blessed with a lot
but I'm not blessed with hair,
so ill hold up my head and
I'll live with the fact,
that when it gets cold
I'll be wearing a hat!

I started to
recede age 25
and aged 29
I shaved my head
for aPlay!
It never grew back.
Slap head, ever since!

LOL

I invited my friend for a 'Netflix and chill'
without an idea what it meant,
(*rumpy, pumpy*)
and then still,
It got very awks (*awkward*)
when they said I was gravy (*great*)
I'm no FWB (*friend with benefits*)
will someone please save me.
This text speak and slang
leaves me out of the crowd.
I said LOL (lots of love)
but it meant 'laugh out loud'
not great when you said it
responding to dan,
who's now on the ward awaiting a scan.

I'm so out of date,
I haven't a clue.
I still use the 8 as a number,
do you?
Is it DM? or IM?
Is it gang or a crew?
Are we BFs or Besties?
Do I, I heart you?
'In my honest opinion' is IMHO,
AFAIK is 'as far as I know'
But what is a FINSTA?
What's shading?
Or snatched?
its all far beyond me
I'm losing this match!

Emojis, emoshe me.
Will someone please coach me?
I don't know my kiss face,
from goblin or ghosty.
There's winkey face,
teary face, tongue out and smiley.
cringe face, heart face,
halo and lying.
Angry face, drooling face,
dizzy and sleepy,
grimace, astonished
bandaged and creepy.
I'll just have to face it,
I don't know what they mean.
I was totally disgraced
with a big aubergine!
Someone sent me a poo!
What is that all about?
I'D WRITE IT IN CAPS
But I don't want to shout.
It's a whole different world
and I'm certainly not there.
I'd rather not bother,
I really don't care,
but I have to keep up,
If I'm going to share,
with the world how I feel,
but it's driving me spare.
I might just switch off,
and go back to my den,
and communicate only
with paper and pen.

Text Speak and Emojis! I hope you understand it, as I didn't!!
LOL (lots of Love) Swalk! (Sealed with a loving Kiss)

Superman

I'm Superman I am.
Superficial, supercritical,
supercilious, super-bad.
Supersensitive, super stupid,
super-silly, super-sad.
Supernormal, super sassy,
superfluous, super-mad.
Yet Supersonic super-love,
supersedes the stupor in us.
Superimposing supernovas,
no supposes it's not over.
Your supernatural superlatives,
supercharge me,
showing true superiority,
supervising a
supersized revival
and imbibing true survival.
You're Wonder Woman you are
and I often wonder why,
you stay with me and never wander,
this wonder makes me fly,
like superman himself,
I rise up, souring high,
giving me a super power,
that grows with every hour.
I know it's now or never,
I'll endeavour to be true.
This love that lies
between you and I
will be our superglue!

This came as a particular challenge to myself, wanting to write a LOVE poem to my wife for our 26th wedding anniversary but without being soppy! I think I achieved that!

Snow

Part of the seasonal theme, but a little humorous nod at temperatures in Devon. We rarely get snow and when we do it never lasts! I'm not complaining though as it's lovely!

So now it's snowing,
the thoughts are growing, of kids playing,
fingers glowing inside toastie gloves
snowballs throwing,
sledges towing
winter heaven
but guess what?
I live in Devon
It's already stopped

Fresh

Last week I made
fresh footprints
in the deep
crunching snow.
This week I walk
on washed through
sand on the warm
Cornish coast.
My lone footprints,
virgin that day
but soon
washed away,
by the rain
and the sea,

Written in the spring, when snow had fallen and yet we also had a trip to the beach! It was one of those lightbulb moments about the fragility of the journey and yet the new opportunities that life brings!

Never to return
but everlasting
through experience
and memory.
I was there,
the first to
walk that route
but evidence
is gone,
yet who knows
which new paths
I will walk tomorrow
and the days to come.

NUDITY

This section could be labelled Life! In all it's rawness. These poems fall into the nudity category! Not literally, but in the sense of the vulnerability and honesty. These are raw, vulnerable and frank poems about life and in some instances my personal life!

One Hundred Years

It's 100 years since those women
said 'No,
we're not doing this anymore
so we will go,
to whatever extremes
that we have now to show,
that all people are equal.
You won't overthrow us
or rule us no more.
We must have our vote
and implore you, to give,
us the rights we deserve.
It's never a problem,
to love and to serve,
but not without choice,
and not when we're
herded in corners,
diverted by orders
that don't make no sense,
or bordered by limits,
surrounded by fences
that don't have a reason.
These naive defences are
nothing but treason
to humanities rights,
we will stand up and fight.
Doing all that it takes to
revive and remake a society,
where there's no bias to people,
 because of their colour ,
their creed or their gender.
This rotten agenda,
forgotten
and rendered quite useless.
We'll choose this new path
where equality reigns,

As our freedom was fought for,
we'll battle again
for the rights of the voiceless,
through struggle and pain,
bringing light to the darkness,
a gentle refrain,
from all that controls us
or tries to unfold us
from unity.
Yes,
we will learn from the boldness
of women and soldiers
who fought for and showed us
together we're stronger.
Our voices no longer not heard.
Our freedom not squandered,
but learning to work
close together for good.
We will be one big family,
as we know that we should be.
Not divided by anger or pride,
or the envy
that causes a war,
and becomes so incendiary
to all that we know
as humanities way.
It's time to be one now
Let's start that today.'

Written for an event
celebrating the centenary
of the suffragettes and also
the end of the 1st world war!

3 Doors Down

I live 3 doors down
from the house 3 doors up.
It's a strange place to see
as the door's never shut.
It stands flung wide open
Inviting to all,
but if you try to approach it
you're greeted by four
of the scariest guards dogs
you ever did see.
Aggressive and violent,
snarling and free
to attack anyone that might
venture too close, so
don't try to enter or visit the host.

The foursome have names
that will give you a clue
as to why they are not friendly
or homely or true.
So please don't approach them
you know you can't touch ,
It's your health you are risking
So don't try your luck.

The first one's called fear
and is tiny but stout,
he shakes in the corner
never wanders about,
seeming lonely and distant
away from the pack,
if you try to get close
he will always attack.

The second's despair,
emaciated and thin

starved of a meal
and empty within.
No future or hope,
she's motionless, numb,
desperate, reactive
and ready to run

The third one's called hatred,
a thug and a beast,
teeth,
sharp as razors,
ready to feast
on anything weak
or frightened
or small.
He's angry and nasty
and up for a brawl.

The fourth one, called failure
has given up the fight,
but don't try to help her,
she's still got a bite.
She's sad and self conscious,
unable to stand,
but attempt to reach out,
you just might lose your hand.

The guard dogs all run riot
not tethered or tamed.
The owner now threatened,
alone and ashamed,
clinging on desperately
to shards of the soul.
What was there to protect
has now gained the
control.

This is a deep and descriptive poem about fear, despair, hatred and failure and some of the issues that we carry around!

Self on the Shelf

When the darkness
gathers round you
and you can't
see any light.
When you feel
you're own
and it's perpetually
night.
When you can't hear
words of guidance
and your life
is feeling numb.
The first thing you should check
Is if your head's
gone up your bum!
You see, self pity is
a nightmare,
self obsession
leaves you lost.
Comparison with others
leaves you counting
your own cost.
Jealousy and bitterness
become your only friends
and pride steps in
reminding you
that it's not fair,
and then,
you're on your own,
quite literally,
you're gone Inside your self.
The only way of getting out,
leave your ego on the shelf.

It's easy to
lose sight of
who you are,
disappearing
up your own
rear end, is
the easiest
way to do
that!

Self pity and
a victim
mentality
can destroy
our true
selves.
As a
performer
I'm well
aware of the
need to let
these things
go.

Just A Man

Laddish, Geezer,
blokey, mate,
stand up, man up
not girly, be straight.

The bossman, the gaffer
no nonsense, tough guy,
handy and manly
be strong now, don't cry.

Grow up, don't show up
those feelings inside.
Speak up, but shut up
all weakness we hide.

Was then
this is now,
we must change with
the times,
but what
makes a man and
what are the signs.

Firm not aggressive,
bold not oppressive,
giving not excessive,
emotive not depressive,
committed not obsessive,
humble but impressive,
classic but progressive,
open and expressive,

Another comment
on society perhaps!

But gently
acknowledging
gender issues!

I couldn't resist the line at the end!
Nice little paradox me thinks!

who am I?
and am I,
allowed
to be me,
or is there
a rule to the man
I should be.
The lines are a blurring.
It's hard now to see.
whats accepted,
expected,
with he and the she.

Maybe the answer,
maybe the key,
Is to be strong and assertive
but gentle and free.
I'll open my heart
and try not to be numb.
Perhaps, the best man I can
be is to be like my mum!

Social Needier

Here we are
on the web,
sharing just how we feel.
Here is me, here's my family,
here's a selfie,
here's a meal.
I am bearing my soul,
this is me being real.
Smiley face,
sad emoji,
all out front,
can't conceal.
I've a need to be wanted,
be accepted and loved.
I've an image to portray,
a profile to construct.
All the while I am hiding
In a real world that's try's
to be true to ourselves
whilst surrounded by lies.
I will be who I think
that you think
I should be!
I'm not sure who that is
Who am I? Who is me?
Do I care just as long

A little insight into my
take on what we
sometimes use social
media for!

as I get lots of likes.
Lots of smiles,
a reaction
It's my need,
my device.
It's my way to be seen
to show just who I am.
Is it there on the surface?
Sincere or a sham?

Am I augmented?
or an avatar?
Am I virtual?
or true?
Am I really being me?
Or should I first
check
with you?

Social media can sometimes be
a tool that encourages self
obsession
and the need for approval.

Fast Lane

Life in the fast lane,
might get you there quicker.
But you don't see the scenery
and the speed makes you sicker.
I'd rather go slower and
take in the view.
Plus the journeys much better
When I take it with you.

I wrote this after
being told that I
drive too fast,
by my wife!

This is for her!

Simple ditty
which says all
that needs to
be said.

The grass isn't
always greener!

The Other Side

They say the
grass is greener
when you get to the other side!
But be careful of hay fever,
which
may get you
once it's died

Anon

Since a very young age,
I've longed to be seen.
To be noticed, acknowledged.
The core of my dream.
The source, being part of a huge family,
the fight for attention
to be noticed as me.
Standing alone in front
of the crowd,
talkative, cheeky,
creative and loud.
I dreamt of the limelight,
standing there proud,
receiving applause
whenever I bowed.
This dream was pursued with
vigour and verve,
happy to lead or happy to serve,
but always believing that
talent would show,
given the chances and
one day be known
by the world,
fame and glory
and dreams now unfurled,
a true winners story
anonymity hurled
by the wayside
and left to wither and die
whist here, popularity
now will reside.
But the truth, is I've tried
and pursued this right through
but not getting to where
I believed I'd get to.

I've spent 20 plus years working in the media and entertainment business, a business that is obsessed with fame and celebrity and being' known'. I've often felt that I may have missed out on opportunities that my ability deserved but was told that I wasn't well known enough because household names sell the show or the programme.

This messed with my self esteem for many years but I now know a God who knows my name and most importantly loves me for who I am.

What more do I need?

opportunities haven't allowed
this to be, whatever the reason,
not many know me.
But I'm not the same guy now,
obsessions have gone
i'm happy to march to
my families song.
Not bow to the self
and live for a lie,
not slave for the chance
To get noticed, then die.

It might be that
passions have faded,
that life's made me jaded,
or rejection invaded
the hope that I had.
Or it might be that actually
I'm glad,
just to focus on things
that will matter,
not grabbing at air
but carefully
caring
for truth
not the glare of the lights
that just blind us and
often divide us.
The power of fame
that clearly denies us of
life with true meaning,
demeaning our value
and leaving
us cold

No I'll boldly proclaim
that i don't need to be known,
by no others, but those
that are waiting at home.
My family, my creator who
has given me hope
and a name that was
founded in heaven.
So whenever I question
my value or worth,
I'll remember the reason
I'm here on the earth,
to celebrate life that is
given by God.
He knows me by name
with a smile and a nod.

Kids

Twenty Two years on
and the child
has flown the nest.
The 2nd heads off soon
and the rest
they say is history,
but history has a knack, you see
of bringing you back to reality.
It's hard to view so far ahead,
let's have some kids we both had said.
And then you see that crowning head
and life just stops you dead
in your tracks and nothing else matters,
all else lacks, and love just
smacks you in the face.
They're yours,
you made them,
that's ace.
But more than that you feel the grace
that offers you this gift of life
that's not bean earned
or bought or strived.
Just lying there helpless,
ready to be taught
to share with,
be with,
from naught
This being that we've brought
into the world
Is ours to nurture,
love and care for.

A poignant and honest piece about empty nest syndrome and being thankful for children!

It makes me cry whenever I perform it!!

Who am I, that I should dare to think
that I have anything to offer these kids,
yet, now I must step up and
be the dad, the man, the one,
who can provide
abide, confide,
reside with them
through thick and thin
and never leave, give in
or be anything but loving and kind.
Cause that's the gift that I've been given
so time to man up,
step up
look up and start living.

And here we are, those years have gone,
the fears, the cheers, the tears are none but
a fleeting memory and here we have
two adults standing there,
who soon will care
for us when we are old
and need the help.
Yet genes and DNA and all
that tells us they are ours
will never be enough to
express and tell the love
that parenthood can give.

And so now it's time for them
to go, to leave,
to grow, to be
the people who
they're meant to be.

Mum

20 years have now passed
and It's hard to believe
that the pain of mum's loss
is still there with me.
As strong as before
but with less memory
but no less the desire though
to talk, touch and see.

My mum was integral
as I guess all mums are,
but unique in the sense of how far
she would go to show
care for the ones
who's families didn't know
how to cope, how to grow,
so they'd come to our home.

I would often wake up
to see we'd expanded,
mum dressing and feeding them all single handed.
Dad would be pastoring churches quite candid
but mum took the lead with the kids that had landed.

The children would come
for a day or a week
which would stretch to a month,
then the family would seek
an extension and sneak
one more child to the fold,
which then led to the spread
of this family so bold.

My most honest and emotional poem to date, about my mum and what an incredible impact she had on many of us, as a foster parent!

My mum died aged 58 and I still miss her terribly, but the impact that she had on so many children and families is her lasting legacy!

The amount short term fostered
were 50 or more, then 3 kids adopted
and 3 who stayed for,
as long as they wanted
until they could leave.
They also had us,
my two brothers and me.

Unconditional love
was bestowed
on us all.
Mum had arms that extended
to big and to small
and never relented to follow the call
of a life that was giving despite of the
gaul,
of perpetual illness
and unending pain,
the effects of arthritis each day and
again
she would never show sadness
or ever complain,
as the children came first
and this was her way.

No judgement was given to colour
or creed,
the focus on loving
whatever the need,
giving hope to the helpless
and sowing the seed
of compassion
and healing in action and deed.
There are many an adult
who owe her their lives,
she rebuilt, reconditioned,
refurbished, revived

the most damaged and broken,
the hurt and deprived,
the ones who were beaten
and barely survived.
Yet my mum built them up
so they flourished and thrived
from the love of a mum
from the day they arrived.

I'm honoured to tell of my mum
and acquaint her to you and recall
there was never complaint
loving difficult children
without a restraint
I know I am biased
but I think mum was a saint.

Home Full

"Do you have any spare change please mate"
he says through wind shattered lips,
akin to Sherpa tensing,
but without the accomplishment.
The eyes speak of many
Everest's not conquered.
The hands speak of harsh winters
and broken dreams.
The clothes speak of poverty
and tobacco
The breath speaks of cheapened liquor
and Colgate less evenings.
"No mate. Sorry". I reply.
But the thoughts don't match the words
as I'm not sorry. No not at all.
I've worked hard for the loose change in my pocket.
The jangle reminds me of early
mornings and long evenings.
The toil, the stress,
the begging for more hours!
Begging!

Now there's a word!
and yet am I really that different
from this tattered man in front of me?
I have a family, so does he, probably,
I have a brain, so does he, definitely,
I have skills and abilities, yep him too.
Perhaps I've been lucky, perhaps!
Perhaps I've made better choices, but
perhaps not.
Perhaps It's just one of those things ,
where it just hasn't worked out for him
and he's not found his best.
or made bad choices
or not had many?

An honest look at
homelessness from a
different perspective!
I was attempting a personal
and honest approach without
being political or preachy!

Are we really that different?
The only difference that I can
see right now,
is that I'm hopeful
and home full
and he's home less.

The Business of Show

The business of show
is a strange thing I know,
It lives for a yes but then kills with a no.
It asks for your heart but your image it
owns, It lifts up your head
but it can't let it go.

When push comes to shove,
it's the pushy that win.
The thick end of the wedge
is quite often the thin.
And the ones that give all
are the ones that are in.
Then you're out of the cold
with a nod and a grin.

For many, the act
covers up the real me.
Not a platform that caters
for true identity.
Just a place to become a big celebrity
But to celebrate what
is not easy to see.
Its a place to enhance,
to advance
and to dance
on the ones that were there
when you first had a chance.

The deep become shallow
then beg you to swim,
on the edge of the coast
where the sharks then begin
to devour the ones who
can't handle the spin
or the lies of the few

They call it Show biz! It's a tough business Often, shallow and raw, breading insecurity from rejection...

...and a business built on image and popularity! But still one I love!

who can brandish the pin
of deflation and failure,
the broken de-railer,
the pressure that says
that there's no one who'll pay ya.

Yet for me there's a freedom
in this show and tell.
If you're born for the spotlight
then light can dispel,
all that falsehood and fable
a chance to be stable
to do all that your able
in being a star.
To show true creation,
to build that foundation
an honest narration
of all that you are.

So I'd rather be honest
and not be a sham,
or court fame and fortune
and build up the dam,
of pretence and deceit
and all thats a scam.
I'm gonna be true
to the person I am.

So ill keep on performing
In true honesty
Not be tied to a system
but open and free,
even if that leads to anonymity.
I am who I am
I'm authentically me.

Prove It

Have you ever made bread?
Just plain
and
simple bread.
It's really very basic,
quite straightforward
like I said.
The ingredients go in,
like yeast and flour
and things.
You mix them all together
but then the real work
it begins.
The dough has to be pummelled.
The whole lot is then
smashed,
It's wrecked and
deconstructed,
totally ruined
then its mashed.
Yes mashed all back together
and repeatedly
again.
It's worked and reworked,
stretched and torn,
It's really quite mundane.
You see,
you're deconstructing
the ingredients.

the gluten activates,
you mess it up
you bring it back,
It moulds then separates.
Divides, then builds
empties and fills
a process of revive,
once killed,
but then its stops,
it's not the end,
It's just start
this break and mend.
Cause now you halt
and let it rest.
It's called the prove!
We prove no less
and in the prove
the dough will rise
Its lifting up,
before your eyes.
The process
has allowed
the dough
from brokeness
to really grow,
without the kneading
nothing works.
This is the proof,
It comes from hurts.

I was watching 'Great British bake off' and bread week. The making of bread
is quite a simple process, however its all in the waiting, the proving.
But that only comes after the pummelling!

62

Nuddie

I've nothing on,
I'm In the buff,
I'm Starkers,
I'm Stripped bare.
Au natural,
the altogether
birthday suit.
right there.
I'm cold and very vulnerable,
no clothes are left to spare.
But It's not of my own doing
But because of Gods true care.
He's removed the rags,
the stuff, the smalls.
The clothes that stank,
with bugs they crawled.
The nasty sins,
the stinky thoughts,
the attitudes, ingratitudes.
The grimy deeds that always
prove,
that all my clothes
need to be new.
The old ones,
God will take away,
so let them go,
give up today.
The rags removed,
no more, they're gone.
New clothes are there.
Just put them on.

Finishing off where
we started. the nudity!

BONUS POEMS

Written on publishing deadline day,
these last two poems sum up this
whole collection well...

Spring Clean

I'm having a spring clean
so I'm keen
to preen and glean inside of me.
But no vacuum machine
will meet these needs.
Mr sheen won't release
or appease the grease
at Easter.
No,
the disease is internal,
so my referral is to
something more
nurturing.
Not virtual,
but soul searching
and eternal.
A power
that can reverse
the brokenness and hurts,
and break the curses,
dispersing
this worsening rot
and stopping the dirt
at the source and not
letting it win.
The cause is often sin,
a word we no longer
like to hint of
but it lingers within,
creating a binful
thats brimful
with waste
that tastes awful
and waits
to devour and turn sour,
deflowering
our innocence,
hindering growth
showering insolence
on all hope of good intentions.
They've become
the unmentionables
as troubles take over
and venture to vent us
of anything tender.
But getting right with Christ
might just bring new signs
of life.
His spiritual knife can cut
out the grime and slime
and in time heal my soul.
I'm
broken, not whole
But only by holding onto
hope through his cross,
that has blotted out this rotten
dross and offered solitude
and wholeness across
the whole of my spirit.
Patrolling perimeters
so this limitless love
can rescind what hinders.
Softening the hardness,
the new light is undimmed,
thinning out darkness,
edges are trimmed.
He's given us life beyond
what we can guess,
cleanliness is pinned to our chest,
the rest will come in heaven.
So bin that, that clings and
stings and come clean
to his throne and own
that which muddies
your heart.
It's time
to begin the clear out
and get a fresh start.

Loosen The Noose

Don't amuse the accuser.
But rather choose to loosen
the noose or you'll lose
all you know
as he pursues
your soul
and bruises ya.
Knowing what
produces hurt in ya
These untruths are abusive
not conducive to growth.
They're loathsome and gross
Choking deep in your throat
Poking fun at your hope
Evoking and promoting brokenness,
and exposing weaknesses.
This bleakness can cheapen
your meaning, demeaning your
freedom.
So flea from believing
you're meaningless
not meant to be.
You are free.
He's seen to that.
So don't be beaten
by that Unreasoning and
low self esteem.
But believe that you've been
planned by the master
craftsman
not accidental
but hand crafted and grafted
Into his plans.
You're life has meaning
and a deepening peace
from the healer will

see through these inaccuracies.
His Beacon will light up
your life inspiring a brightness
that banishes frightening
falsehoods, enlightening
wholesome truth.
Pursuing new grooves
of who you really are.
You are more than the sum of your
parts
so start
believing
what's true in that heart
of yours.
Ensue authenticity
with God's synchronicity
removing what's fake
and making new
with these basic truths.
You are loved
You didn't choose this,
It chose you
and found you exactly where you are
You are forgiven
A gift that's given freely,
not needing anything but your heart.
You are not alone,
you are precious
and being honed.
Heaven's love has met us
and shown blessings
beyond measure.
Our Heavenly Father
Is waiting patiently
to welcome us home.